Our Mama is a Beautiful Garden

By Katy Tessman Stanoch

Illustrated by Jessica Bailey

For Maxwell and Louis ~ the true heroes of this story.
I love you bigger than the sky.
K.T.S.

For Nana and Mema,
two of the most beautiful gardens I know.
J.B.

Text copyright © 2013 by Katy Tessman Stanoch
Illustrations copyright © 2013 by Jessica Bailey
Edited by Rosemary Wellner
Layout by Nicki McCracken (sixonetwo.com)

ISBN 9780615784083

Rhythmelodic Books
Post Office Box 1071
Minnetonka, MN 55345

www.rhythmelodic.com/mamasgarden

A Note from the Author

During my diagnosis and treatment for breast cancer, I tried to find a book I could read to my children to help them understand what was happening to me. I wanted a book that instilled hope and explained the basics of cancer. I never found that book.

When I was explaining each step of my surgeries and treatments to my sons, I discovered a theme: Cancer is a bad weed in my garden. There are many ways to weed a garden. To rid our garden of weeds, we prefer pulling them rather than spraying them. Cancer treatments usually require both surgery and chemotherapy. Taking medicine that made me sick was hard for my boys to comprehend and difficult to explain. The garden analogy made it easier for them to understand.

Breast cancer is the most common cancer in women worldwide. America has 2.5 million breast cancer survivors, the largest group of cancer survivors in the U.S. It affects one in eight women and of those women one-third are between the ages of 20 and 49. Early detection is key, which is why most doctors recommend that women at the age of 40 start receiving regular mammograms. Many of these women have young children in their lives. (Statistics come from the Susan G. Komen Foundation website.)

I'm confident that having my sons tell our family story will give other families the strength, courage, and optimism they need during an awful time that can feel quite hopeless.

My name is Louis and this is my little brother, Maxwell. When I was 6 and Maxwell was 3, our Mama got real sick with breast cancer.

We don't like breast cancer.

Mama is a singer. All day long, she sings. She knows songs about the change of seasons, songs about sunshiny days, even when it's not, and songs about people with silly names.

I like to pretend my name is John Jacob Jingleheimer Schmidt.

Mama always sees the bright side of things and the silver lining.

Mama is also a hugger. Some days, it's like she's hugging me all the time! Her hugs always make me feel good and she sings gently in my ear. She makes up her own songs, singing something like, "You're fantastic."

Mama's hugs are tight and soft.

We love being outside, hiking in the woods and helping Mama in the garden.

Red flowers are my favorite.

One day, Mama came home from her doctor checkup and told us she was sick, but that it was not a sickness we could catch from her. She said she had a disease called breast cancer. Cancer? It sounded so scary.

Cancer sounded so scary.

The doctor called cancer a tumor that was growing in Mama's body. Mama explained to us that cancer is like a really bad weed in her garden. It had to be taken out of her body right away.

This weed made me very mad and sad.

My brother and I were so mad, Gramma and Grampa gave us a
big clown to punch. Whenever we were upset, we'd punch him.
It sure made me feel better.

He fell over when I hit him.

Mama said it would be okay if Auntie gave us foam swords to use with the blow-up clown. It was fun to knock him down because he'd pop right back up again.

To remove the weed, Mama had a surgery called a mastectomy, where the doctor removed both of her breasts. She had to stay in the hospital for three days and two nights.

We were so happy when she got home. But she didn't have any energy to sing to us.

She looked different.

We were so lucky
Gramma and Grampa
could come to take care
of us while Daddy took
care of Mama.

Gramma knows how I like
my school lunches.

Grampa knows how
to have fun.

When Mama was all healed from her surgery, she was strong enough
to start special medicine treatments called chemotherapy, chemo for short.
This medicine kills the cancer cells that Mama calls weed seeds.

Cancer cells, or weed seeds, might have been released inside Mama's body.

I wanted all the weed seeds dead and gone.

These weed seeds are like burrs in a garden that can float around and stick to things.

Burrs get inside my socks and poke me. Ouch!

Mama explained to us that the medicine made sure the cancer weed seeds would never take root in her body again.

The chemo medicine made Mama real sick. She said this was part of getting well. How strange! I didn't understand that.

I didn't like it when Mama was sick.

The chemo treatments took all day. It was hard to be at school when I was so worried about Mama.

Gramma and Grampa played doctor with me.

Mama was so sick, she couldn't sing her songs during the day, and her lullabies at night were very short.

Daddy would sing to us, but he knows different songs.

The chemo made Mama's hair fall out. She said that shaving all her hair off made her feel hopeful, just like putting a garden to bed for the winter and looking forward to new flowers in the spring.

Mama let Gramma shave it all off!

Mama said that the last time she was bald was when she was born.
Do you think she looked like that when she was a baby?

I think she looked like bald Daddy.

Her voice was the same, though, and she sang the same songs to us.

"Puff the Magic Dragon" sounded the same
when we were cozy in bed.

A lot of people wanted to help. Some
brought us suppers, like beef stroganoff
and sloppy joes with potato chips.

I loved the desserts.

Daddy and I set the table and talked
about everyone who loves us.

We drew lots of pictures for Mama, and she got cards in the mail almost every day. I liked watching her smile when she opened them.

I got to tape them up on the walls.

Some women who have cancer need to have radiation. That's when a super-strong light is focused on where the cancer tumor or weed was growing.

Mama didn't need this.

The cancer weed does not like the light, and the cancer weed is destroyed. It makes me think of how just the right amount of sunshine makes a garden more healthy.

Mama had reconstruction. This is a big word for the repair Mama chose for her body. This process made her very uncomfortable for a while.

I had to hug her gently.

Mama and Gramma would talk about Mama going to see a doctor to get a "fill." Mama said the doctor put mini-pillowcases under her skin in her chest. She would get them filled to restore her original shape. The cancer weed cannot grow in her new breasts.

I wanted her big hugs again.

Mama was tired and needed to rest. We spent a lot of time on the couch reading books. Mama's favorite books to read were about courage and hope.

I liked books about superheroes.

When Mama was all done with the chemo treatments and reconstruction surgeries, her energy and hair started coming back.

It was fun to tug on her hair and it didn't come out.

Her hair was a different color than before, but that didn't matter.

We were so happy when Mama was feeling better and our life was back to normal. She told us her body—her garden—was healthy again.

We planted new flowers in our yard.

Mama told us we are her heroes and that helped make her garden beautiful again.

Our Mama is a beautiful garden.

Acknowledgments

Being diagnosed with breast cancer was like falling down a deep dark hole; there were times I didn't think I'd reach the bottom. When I finally did, the love, prayers, gifts, and good vibes that were sent my way created a strong, sturdy ladder that gave me the ability to climb out.

I am blessed to have such a supportive sister, Caryl Mousseaux, who went down that hole and pushed me up the ladder. I am appreciative of my fantastic brother, Bill Tessman, and sister-in-law, Landi Sones-Tessman, who had weekly playdates with our boys.

Words cannot properly express how grateful I am to Mom and Dad (Charon and Bill Tessman) for being there for us so completely and selflessly throughout my whole journey.

My ladder of support had many steps including my wonderful relatives, neighbors, and friends who gave so many gifts of meals, books, fruit baskets, flowers, and chocolate. Thanks to my girlfriends Kelly Sanches, Jennifer Hernandez, and Kelley Mayer who always made sure I had plenty of Laugh Therapy. I am lucky to have the support of my dear friend, Nicki McCracken, who sat by my side for so many hours in the chemo room. And thanks to my "secret admirer" who sent me anonymous notes and gifts. (I still don't know who you are.)

My outstanding medical care givers at Methodist's Park Nicollet Cancer Center gave me the confidence and comfort I needed to carry on.

Thanks to Kate Bailey and Elli Rader for asking me to be a part of Of Scars, everyone at Hope Chest for Breast Cancer and Patterson Dental (especially Jennifer Hannon) for sharing my story, and Barbara Porwit for including me in her Breast Cancer Superheroes portrait series. Special thanks to The Children's Theatre Company in Minneapolis for honoring Louis and Maxwell, naming them Young Heroes, recognizing how they faced their mama's breast cancer with the courage only a true-to-life hero has.

I have deep appreciation for Jessica Bailey who offered her artistic talents so generously and for Rosemary Weller and Nicki McCracken for sharing their excellent editing and design skills. I am grateful to my wonderfully helpful neighbor and friend, Nancy Powell, who believes in the importance of this book.

This journey is a road well traveled. Thanks to my Breast Friends for being the Warriors they are: Judy Erdahl, Jan Graziani, Pat Willenbring, Grace Folkerds, Jackie Thompson, Deanna Thompson, Kathy Arnold, Georgina Graper Moore, Mari Sikkink, Diane Erickson, Terri Joski-Lang, Molly Maher, Kevyn Burger, Colleen Liz Donley, Aasne Daniels, Virginia LeBlanc, Katrina Haas Dohm, Kathy Knoblauch, Sarah Brown, Jill Gause, Julie Maanum, Janet Neau, Alexia Glassco, Marti Swanson, and Karen Ege.

Special praise to my Semi-Colon Warrior Brothers Mark Shirmacher and Scott Barton-Smith and my Grandma Ethel Tessman, Auntie Lois Bader, and Auntie Alice Jane Moat, who have braved the fight so heroically.

Special thanks to my darling husband, Dave, for giving me a tiara on my 40th birthday.

The heroic guts and glitz our sons, Louis and Maxwell, displayed during this journey is profoundly inspiring. For that, I thank them with everything I've got.

– K.T.S.

About the Author

PHOTO: ALISON LEA

After her first mammogram, in 2009, Katy Tessman Stanoch was diagnosed with breast cancer. She had a double mastectomy on her fortieth birthday, endured eight chemotherapy treatments in 14 weeks, and underwent several reconstruction surgeries. Katy's sons, Louis and Maxwell, were only ages 6 and 3 at the time of her diagnosis.

Katy is a full-time mom who is an active volunteer at her boys' school and teaches early childhood music family classes. Her husband, David Stanoch, is a musician and educator. Together, Dave and Katy perform and record her original music. Katy has a BA from Minnesota State University Moorhead and has worked as a communications contractor for a variety of businesses in the Twin Cities.

The family's love of nature helped Louis and Maxwell understand the changes going on with their mother's body. They visit the Northern woods of Minnesota regularly and volunteer year-round at their local nature center.

Katy and her family live in Minnetonka, Minnesota.

PHOTO: DANA BAILEY

About the Illustrator

After studying Visual Arts at the University of Texas at Dallas, Jessica Bailey graduated from Eugene Lang College The New School for Liberal Arts in New York City with a degree in Literary Studies.

Currently, Jessica resides in Minneapolis, Minnesota. When she's not illustrating, Jessica embraces her passion for children's books at her job at the famed Wild Rumpus Bookstore.